*always
Brenda God...
Romans 8:28*

Alayna

*a Tribute to Courage and Destiny
in a Life Never Lived*

Brenda Godson

All scripture quotations are taken from the New American Standard Version of the Bible, unless otherwise noted. Scripture quotations taken from the New American Standard Bible®, Copyright © 1960, 1962, 1963, 1968, 1971, 1972, 1973,1975, 1977, 1995 by The Lockman Foundation. Used by permission. (www.Lockman.org)

Scripture marked (AMP) are quotations taken from the Amplified® Bible, Copyright © 1954, 1958, 1962, 1964, 1965, 1987 by The Lockman Foundation. Used by permission. (www.Lockman.org)

This is a

DIMENSIONS / MINISTRIES

www.jackrtaylor.com
Production

Published by

Burkhart Books

www.burkhartbooks.com
Bedford, Texas

Dedications

My husband and I would like to dedicate this book to our daughter Amanda and her husband Nick. Through their faith and love for each other in the face of adversity, they modeled to a world the ability to overcome and walk in grace through trying times.

Also to those who consistently prayed for our family. May each of you know that your prayers warmed us during times of great vulnerability and grief. We offer a special thank you to my parents and sister for driving in from Texas on a moment's notice to provide comfort and support, and to others who rose to the call of prayer and brought meals and lessened the load.

To Teresa Watkins, I thank you for calling me on a day when exhaustion had totally taken over and for your offer to pray for me the entire time I slept, not leaving your post until I awakened. To Shirley Vaughan and Teresa who texted me minute by minute, day after day to receive strategic prayer points and offer validation to deep feelings as I processed them, never passing judgment or devaluing my feelings or concerns.

To Donna Arenella for being available at the Hospital during those hardest hours.

To my son Mathew for standing with his sister during those days in the hospital and to employers who extended grace, when things were left undone.

Most importantly to God for being ever present in our midst.

Contents

Dedications	3
Foreword	7
Preface	11
Introduction	13
Prologue	17
Chapter 1	23
Chapter 2	26
Chapter 3	32
Chapter 4	41
Chapter 5	51
Chapter 6	58
Chapter 7	68
Chapter 8	73
Chapter 9	75
Chapter 10	84
Chapter 11	91
About Amanda & Nick	101

Foreword

When I read the manuscript for the following pages, my memory went back to a dream, a sad dream come true.

In that dream, when my oldest son was still a young toddler who had just started to walk, my husband and I were taking a stroll in the woods with our son holding my hand. Then at an instantaneous moment he broke lose and started to run ahead. Not being familiar with the area, I ran after him and called him back and instructed him to stay beside us. After my husband and I entered into a focused discussion, we did not notice that our son was no longer with us. When I called for him, I did not get an answer until all of a sudden I heard him call for help. I ran in the direction where the voice came from and saw him in the middle of an area filled with quicksand. I tried to reach him but was unable because of the distance. I looked for a limb to hand to him to take a hold of so that I could pull him out. By the time I had found a limb to offer him, he had slipped further away. Now I looked for a longer limb. When I found one, I again faced the same problem until I had to watch my son disappear under the sand while I was help-lessly standing by and unable to save him.

That dream was so strong that it seemed real. When I awoke I jumped up to check on my son and found him sound asleep.

I did not pay any attention to that dream and said to myself that it was just a dream...until 19 years later that dream would tragically become true with my son taking his own life.

All of us have experienced losses, similar but not exactly the same, with enough commonalities to invoke sympathy in us all for one another.

There is, however a stark contrast in the way Brenda and Amanda walked through their crisis. They had a faith to hold them up; I had none.

Brenda's story stirred that old memory in me and made me wonder how I would handle it now.

This story is a tribute to faith with a determination to walk through the night with hope and an anticipation of a new day.

Thank you, Amanda for holding on to hope, and Brenda, for journaling the whole story. You have helped us now and through future days.

Friede Taylor
Vice President, Dimensions Ministries
Melbourne, Florida

Preface

We have been blessed with the privilege of journeying through life with Brenda and Joe alongside us for quite a few years now. The entire Godson family occupies a very special place in our hearts. We often analyze things that happen to us, our family or close friends and deposit them into one of two groups of thought. This is good or this is bad. The "good" things we rejoice in and the "bad" we lament as it usually brings sadness and/or pain, often coupled with the question "why?"

Alayna Renee's story is a perfect example of this on both accounts. Though her little body never drew a breath of air, she was always alive and in the palm of God's hand, her Creator. She touched lives from within and continues to touch lives from heaven even at this very moment. The Kingdom of God is so much more than we can imagine, dream or comprehend. So "why?"

Alayna? Some answers may come in due time and the answers will be astounding to our minds, hearts and spirit.

This story is about God's love and His goodness and choosing to find Him in every moment. Penned on the wings of such great revelation, we believe the words written by Brenda's hand are truly expressions of God's heart. The title says it all—the words on these pages will release courage and destiny to the multitudes!

John and Shirley Vaughan
Waves of Fire Ministries

Introduction

I read this arresting story when I first received the manuscript. I had to read it again, weeping through most of it as I had read it at first. Touched with the gripping and splendidly written coverage of the perfect storm with multiple faces, I winced again and again as the tragic realization dawned that the young mother's first pregnancy was to end with the baby still in her womb. The author is my trusted Personal Assistant of many years. I have known every member of this family during the time we have worked together.

This splendidly written narrative is about a life that was lost before it was lived, with a beating heart and given a name, Alayna. She was sung to and prayed for and her parents and grandparents were thrilled at the prospects of holding her and watching her grow up. They anticipated little-girl ways, playing with her hands, softly cooing to her newly-discovered world, going to school, playing with her cousins and growing eventually and too soon into a lovely lady.

It was not to be so with Alayna. She would never take her first breath outside her mother's body. She would die a few weeks before her scheduled arrival, fiercely loved and eagerly awaited by all of this wonderful family.

It is a remarkable happening when someone, caught in a perfect storm on multiple fronts, is able to keep centered in reality while being crushed in the vortex of the swirling winds of tragedy. That someone was the grandmother, the mother of the mother, the author of these pages. This family rooted in faith and grounded in the truths of Scripture, stood firm in the face of horrific circumstances, each one's faith bolstering the others'.

One who has not walked through the loss of a loved one never quite understands the crosswinds of such a storm, the inner stirrings of a powerful love suddenly facing a dead end, multiplied when it is a mother who loses a child and, to increase the pain, bearing a dead child inside her. Labor pains, normally accepted as promises of a new life, now stabbing reminders of a life ended too soon, nourished by a mother's fierce instincts.

This is the story of a life that never lived, and yet baby Alayna will influence an ever-widening crowd all the years of the future. It is the story of a bold and daring young mother who never suspected her inner capacities to respond with such faith and fortitude that pleasingly stunned all around her in this saga. But Amanda, that young mom, would walk out of the storm only to discover she was plagued with Cystic Fibrosis, a feature of grief compounded. But stand she did, and continues!

This book is the story of a mother, Brenda, Amanda's mother whose grief was escorted by her own helplessness to prevent the looming crises and all the while taking mental notes that would form this treatise the reader is holding right now. Many readers, caught in the grip of similar losses and disappointments, will take heart from Brenda's courage to pen this testimony.

This is the story of a family, brought together by tragedy which, when the clouds began to gather, would stand together, each making the other stronger and better. Joe, father and grandfather, ever firm and encouraging in his unshaken faith and love. Nick, the husband and father, showing what tenderness and thoughtful love really is.

Life is a strange mixture of midnight and sunshine, grief and gladness, pain and delight, tragedy and triumph, the latter always winning out at the end of the day. The last verse of this otherwise sad song brings delight to all, heralding a new day. A new life is introduced into the world, Alayna's cousin, Phoebe, born a few days afterward to Amanda's brother, Matthew, and Lisa, his wife.

You will find that the record of this story will move you, whether you find yourself in a similar struggle or not. If you find yourself in such a dire strait, you will be moved and inspire even more to rise to the standard set by this gallant family in such trying times.

Thank you, to the Godson clan, and thanks again, Brenda, for giving us something we can touch and hold and remember—a story well told, a map through stormy days we will all need one day ourselves—and cannot forget.

A final note from all of us who witnessed and walked together through the night: "Alayna Renee Wilson, we will see you later, a stunningly beautiful sight!

Jack R. Taylor
President, Dimensions Ministries
Melbourne, Florida

Prologue

Nick and Amanda found each other at a time when they thought dreams had faded.

Nick, who had always worked towards a life long career in the service, found that his job field was being dissolved and received a early termination. He quickly enrolled in school to take advantage of the GI Bill. In a short time, saddled with the disappointment of unrealized childhood dreams, he made his way back home to Florida to regroup, taking a part time job at 7-11.

Amanda had always dreamed of being a wife and mother. In her eyes, that was the greatest honor one could have. Her conversations were filled with lessens and principals she had picked up along the way that would help her foster the best family environment she could one day. Because it was her deepest hearts desire, she experienced many failed relationships, never able to find that perfect someone who had the same dreams in mind. Eventually she settled into a job at 7-11, to work and wait for that perfect somebody.

Within a week of Nick coming on the scene at 7-11, he began coming to church. Everyone liked him immediately. He was kind, gentle and thoughtful. It was obvious that he was interested in our daughter, but because she had been so wounded in previous relationships, her eyes were not focusing in on the new landscape.

A few weeks later, I was going to Walgreens to pick out a mother's Day card after church, and standing on the isle in front of the cards, was Nick, picking a card out for his mother. He seemed a little sad and I went up and hugged him.

He began to tell me about his interest in my daughter and how the moment he saw her he knew she had to be a part of his life forever. He explained that he would love to have her in his life as his girl, but if he could only have her as a friend, she needed to be a best friend.

My heart melted at the tenderness by which he spoke of her. How he smiled when he thought of her dancing in the isles of the store at work, singing as she put away candy. He shared how cute and contagious she was, that quickly she had them both singing and dancing in the aisle.

In the next week or so, Nick brought up his violin and began playing with our church praise team. No one knew what to expect as he opened the case to his instrument and rosined the bow. I could only imagine if he played the song of his heart, it would be beautiful.

We positioned him next to our daughter who was playing the keyboard. One, two three the sound came forth from the heart of a gentle man, full of tender compassion and depth. I stood in awe as I encountered the heart of this young man as he played.

Later that day as we arrived home, my daughter spoke of the beauty she saw in his gift and how there was something different about this young man. She agreed to see him as friends, because she was still in shell shock over the past. Within a month, they were in a full dating relationship.

The two were so happy. Life was as it should be. For the first time in either of their lives, they were experiencing love in action. They were giddy and lively, finding that they had so many things in common.

For the first time my daughter had found someone to share her life, her interest and even her faith with. She had a man, not a boy, who loved family, enjoyed the simplicities of life and did not pressure her from a position of a hormone driven mentality. He was real and she could be real with him.

Within a few months, Nick proposed. For eight months, wedding plans were underway. Past failings and unrealized dreams were but a blur, because now a whole new hope of a future was in full view.

Nick utilized his VA benefits and bought them a beautiful home, a month before they married. He lived in it, preparing it with the help of his bride to be, until she could finally join him once they were married.

A wedding took place and it was beautiful. It was held at an old colonial home in Old Town Cocoa, Florida. They took a week long honeymoon in the mountains and had a glorious time. We were all overjoyed, both families alike, that our children had finally found their lifelong soul mates.

Things could not have been better for them. Nick had landed a promising job and was making almost as much as my husband and was still only 24 years old. My daughter also went from working in a convenience store, to working in a corporate office building.

They took a cruise and a few other trips, enjoying a time of great blessing. Within the first year, they both agreed that there was so much love between them they were ready to start growing their family.

It was decided they would allow things to happen naturally. They would not prevent pregnancy, but would not work at it like it was a job or duty to be performed. They simply left it in God's hands to bless them whenever the time was right.

It took some months, but finally, one day, the news came…and they announced, "WE ARE PREGNANT!"

Chapter 1

After five years of trials, peace and joy had finally become our song. The personal devastation of the war in Afghanistan left our oldest son disconnected from family due to extreme Post Traumatic Stress Syndrome. Joe and I had finally come to a place of total reliance on God to bring about reconciliation and healing to his mind and heart one day. As a family, we had arrived at the belief that things would be reconciled in God's time, and that our miracle was fast approaching. We came to a place where we could lay down concern for what our eyes were seeing and embrace that which had yet to be seen, by faith.

Christopher Columbus wrote, *"You can never cross the ocean unless you have courage to lose sight of the shore."*

We found that we must be willing to leave situations on the shore of our fears in order to sail away to new horizons. It is difficult to lay down our own efforts at trying to fix or restore, because it feels like we are leaving behind a situation to die. Taking our hands off of it, meant relinquishing our need to have it the way it's always been. It meant that we trust the End from the Beginning no matter what it looks like down the road.

I assure you, most solemnly I tell you,
unless a grain of wheat falls into the earth
and dies, it remains just one grain; it never
becomes more, but lives by itself alone.
But if it dies, it produces many others
and yields a rich harvest.
John 12:24 (AMP)

Multiplication requires death. If we want to see an increase in relationships between ourselves and others, or ourselves and God, we must be willing to let the grains of our ways, the grains of our efforts, the grains of our will, the grains of our needs, fall to the ground and die.

But nothing ever really dies when it is placed in the hands of God. We knew our son, if left in God's capable hands, would one day be reunited with his family, either here or on the other side of eternity. Our fears of never seeing him again had to be left behind or we would forever be held captive by the pain and suffering of deferred hope.

Hope deferred makes the heart sick,
but a longing fulfilled is a tree of life.
Proverbs 13:12

I would never want anyone to assume that our longing for him has ended. A part of us always looks, always hopes and always believes for his return; however, we are no longer held captive by the fruitless works of pain and fear of never seeing him again.

Chapter 2

While our hearts were breaking over the separation between us and our son, our other two children were joyfully stepping in to their dreams. Our son Matt was in the process of finishing Paramedic training and was on his way to the Fire Academy. He and his wife had their third child on the way and were celebrating the excitement of finally getting their girl in the mix of two older brothers.

My daughter Amanda and her husband Nick, who had tried for some time to get pregnant, were blessed to find out that not only were they pregnant, but she was carrying a girl, too. Two granddaughters on the way—what a blessing!

Baby rooms were decorated and painted, ultrasounds made, baby clothes bought and gifts of t-shirts given to the mommies for them to wear as billboards on their bulging bellies. These babies were to come within a month of each other and this family was celebrating it in all grand style.

Around the six month of pregnancy, my daughter's OBGYN began to notice that my daughter wasn't gaining weight. We were not concerned because she never got beyond a size 1 ever. We just figured she was a small girl and therefore would have a small baby. She did, however, struggle with a problem of allergies all her life.

From the moment she was born, we remember her having a stuffy nose. By the time she was three months old, she had already had pneumonia twice. At three months, she was in the hospital. A few days had gone by and we had her transferred into another hospital that had a better children's wing. Upon arrival we were informed that had we not gotten her there when we did, she would have been dead within 24 hours.

All through her precious life, we were back and forth to doctors, told it was just a severe case of allergies. From one allergy medication to the next, we followed the leading of her doctors and still she would end up getting an infection that required antibiotics. She was healthy in every other way. She took dance, participated in girl scouts, ran, played and did everything else a girl her age did.

Now, because she was pregnant, the allergies became worse. Her OB suggested that this may be a problem until she delivers and recommended allergy medication throughout her time to control onset of infection. At the six month point of pregnancy she developed pneumonia and was forced to take a series of antibiotics.

Protein drinks were recommended to assist in weight gain, because at six and a half months, she was only measuring the equivalent of a normal 5 and 1/2 months of pregnancy. The antibiotics were not working, so they extended the regimen. She was also sent to a high risk OB to monitor fetal growth.

Medicine has come a long way over the years. So much can be seen by ultrasound observation. Ultra sounds were done every week and Doppler readings were done to track blood flow to the baby. Doppler readings are fascinating, because through these tests they are able to see blood traveling from the placenta into the umbilical cord and from there to the baby. They can tell if the volume is correct and even listen to the pulse of the blood coming through the cord. Once it enters the baby, you can see how blood gets to the heart and then pumps its way through each of the organs. It is truly fascinating to see the handiwork of God, functioning as it is intended to function.

For you created my inmost being;
you knit me together in my mother's womb.
I praise you because I am fearfully
and wonderfully made;
your works are wonderful,
I know that full well.
                    Psalm 139:13-14

All continued to go well even with the diagnosis of a bilateral uterus and concerns for growth restriction because of it. We were told early on that my daughter had a bilateral uterus. That meant that she didn't have a completely open womb like most women. She had a Y shaped uterus. The good news was that both chambers were open to each other with blood flowing between each. Sometimes women with a bilateral uterus have a complete wall between each side, but my daughter only had a partial wall, so it was believed that she could still have a safe pregnancy. It did indicate that she might have some issues with restrictions on the baby as she grew.

We loved seeing our granddaughter every week on the sonograms. We could see her every little body movements on the screen and even the movement of her lips when she made little pouty faces. We were getting to know her everyday and loving her more by the minute. Being sent home for another week with good reports was exciting.

The baby was now at 31 weeks and if the need to take her early arose, she could easily survive outside of the womb with little assistance, if any. Each day was a blessing.

On the other front, our son's wife was doing well with her pregnancy, too. Mommy was getting bigger by the day, and upon first glance, it looked like she could deliver any day, though she still had over a month to go. Everyday, I was thanking God that our long suffering had come to an end at least for a season. We were entering into a time of extreme excitement and joy upon the arrival of our two granddaughters, Alayna and Phoebe.

Our children were so blessed, each owned their own home and were able to totally rely on the provisions that God had so graciously provided through good jobs and promising careers. This family had undergone a very difficult season that actually spanned over 8 years, but now we believed we were about to enjoy a time of rest from the extreme adversity and know real joy that is too often take for granted.

Chapter 3

The time came for my daughter, Mandy's, long awaited baby shower. She was now seven months pregnant and was feeling the baby move often. Many friends and family attended to bless her on that Sunday afternoon. She received so many wonderful gifts that it took an hour and a half just to open them all. One of her friends made numerous items with baby Alayna's name appliquéd on them. Burp rags, onesies and other clothing. A baby blanket was hand made by one of her childhood friends and we all delightfully rejoiced at the sight of each little thing. Bottles and pacifiers hung from clothes lines inside and games were played to include even the men in the room. It was truly a joyful day and soon Alayna would be here and we would be able to see her in all of her tiny little outfits.

Mandy would probably change her numerous times a day, just to see her sporting another cute look. She had ordered headbands to match every outfit and she had even bought some little black and white converse tennis shoes to match her mommy's and daddy's. The only chance this child had of ever wearing each of the multitude of outfits hanging in the closets and folded in drawers was if her mommy played dress up a few times every day. We were so blessed by loving friends who celebrated the coming of this new life with us.

After the Shower, things were picked up, all the gifts loaded in my daughter's and son-in-law's SUV and everyone headed for home. My daughter and her husband decided to wait until the next day to unload everything, because it had been a long and exciting day and they were tired and work came in the morning, so they went immediately to bed that night.

Monday morning came after a short night of sleep and both rose to prepare for work. My daughter came out of the bathroom to tell her husband that she was spotting and admitted she was afraid.

Mandy was never afraid of much of anything. During the pregnancy, she diligently did everything that was recommended, but never did she allow fear to enter her mind. She lived by Matthew 6:34 – Therefore don't worry about tomorrow, for tomorrow will worry about itself. Each day has enough troubles of its' own.

This was a fearless girl. Once when she was 18 years old, she drove her car all the way from Florida to DC, never stopping for a break. We received a call from my brother saying she had arrived and all the while we thought she was at work. I remember asking my husband, what would make her launch out like that, a young girl on the road who had never been out of the small town where we lived and venture out to a possibly dangerous place she had never been before, all by herself. His reply was, "she is her mother's daughter. I remember someone who took off to Africa by themselves once." Quickly, I made the connection. We were both fearless, and if she could ever redirect that courage in a positive way, she could have a great impact on everyone else around her, but until then we prayed for God to protect her from herself.

Mandy and Nick decided they should go to the hospital to have things checked out. My husband and I meet them there. A nurse came in and listened to her belly and became very concerned as she was unable to hear the baby's heartbeat.

A huge wave began building inside of each of us as we pushed back negative thoughts. I convinced myself that there is no way we would come this far and end up losing our granddaughter. All my daughter had ever wanted to be was a wife and a mother. She dreamed about it her whole life. There was no way that God would allow my daughter to lose her baby and have to watch her brother have his baby in less than three weeks. There was no way God would allow this not even 12 hours after her baby shower.

At the moment we begin to perceive life and God that way, we find ourselves in a heap of trouble. When we presume to know what God will and won't allow, we take over as creator to write history with our own twist on it. This is a dangerous place to be, because we do not know the beginning from the end, and therefore we falsely qualify ourselves to know what is best. We set ourselves up to be drastically disappointed when our plans and views fail to meet our expectations.

God tells us that His ways are higher than ours, that they are different from ours and therefore, we are best positioned to take a passengers view of the journey.

I can remember a dream I had about two weeks before this whole thing unfolded. I dreamed I was in a car and my spiritual father, Jack Taylor was driving. I was leaning over from the passenger side resting near his armpit as he had his arm wrapped around me. When I awakened, I asked God about the dream and I felt him tell me that he was taking me on a journey to a destination unknown, but that he had me tucked up under his loving arm and I would rest as we went along.

Go figure...God was aware of this whole thing and had me right where he wanted me!

The ultrasound tech came in and carefully powered up the machine. I found myself becoming aggravated by the length of time it was taking for the stupid thing to come on line. I know that it was misguided impatience, but my emotions were revving up. Finally, the machine was ready after 10 minutes of preparation and the pictures were displayed on the screen.

Beautiful baby Alayna with little hands, little feet, sweet little nose, little rib cage, and perfect little heart lay still and lifeless before my eyes. I knew before anything was said. I had seen her each week and watched what the technicians observed. I had learned to recognize the four chambers of her heart and how they moved with blood entering in and out, pushing supply to the rest of her healthy little organs. Now on the screen, her heart lay lifeless and still. No blood in and no blood out. Four perfect chambers lay still as if a photo snapshot had been taken of them. There was no animation.

I looked around at the faces of my daughter, and both of our husbands, each awaiting the results of what the tech was seeing, but I already knew. The death sentence had been read in the deepest place of my heart before a human word was ever spoken. As the words came from the tech, "I'm sorry she's gone", all hearts sank in unison. This perfect little baby who we had just seen lively and moving on Wednesday, who had just received gifts that would provide for all her needs, still in the back of mommy and daddies SUV, was now gone. Everything in a matter of moments was ripped from our hearts by the dagger of reality and nothing but God himself could change it.

I heard it said once that, "God puts a sword to your chest and says come here."

Bill Johnson preached a message about God's desire to arm an army to be mercy givers. He talked about those that need vindication or have to be right as those living out of a poverty of heart. He states how Solomon was called to build a temple because God knew he would make the right choices and how upon completion of the temple, he offered a sacrifice.

I have seen over the years everything from complacency to pain. Tragedy strikes a person or family and others remain distant, continuing on with life without missing a beat. They acknowledge the suffering, but wouldn't dream of climbing down in the ditch of deep despair to help them walk out. They have the belief that God would not expect them to stop their lives and its activities to embrace someone else's tragedy, especially in that place where there is nothing in it for the person whose life is happy and hopeful. Because grief and loss are not attractive and only stand to dampen the moment of someone else's joy, they quickly avoid face to face contact with it and carry on with feeding their own need for the good part of life. That is not to say that there aren't those that try, but just don't have the words to express their deep felt sympathies. If we really took a long hard look at it, we would probably find that no one wants to exchange happy for sad.

Rejoice with those who rejoice; mourn with those who mourn.
Romans 12:15

We think that it has to be either/or, but in the Kingdom, sometimes it is both/and. In order to embrace the full measure of the Kingdom, we must be able to embrace the full measure of the heart of the Father.

The question becomes, "what will I do in the face of other's pain"? Will my heart be one of humility and mercy? Will I offer a sacrifice for those in need out of my place of plenty?

These are the questions that confronted me following this horrible moment in the life of my family.

Chapter 4

The doctor came in and explained that though the baby had passed my daughter would still have to go through the full birthing process. That was something that she had been nervous about because this was her first child. She was now confronted with having to go through labor six weeks before she was emotionally prepared, as well as the immediate reality of the tremendous loss of her baby.

She was placed in a room at the end of the hall in the labor and delivery department of the hospital. A Pitocin drip was started to induce labor. We knew this would take some time, because she was not even prepped for delivery. She still had over six weeks to go before the baby was due.

The emotional pain from the grief of the loss was overwhelming. The physical pain began with contractions within an hour of the drip being started. Her oxygen level was checked and found to be low, but it was not surprising due to her extreme congestion from lingering pneumonia. The nurses came and removed the baby heart monitor and the contractions monitor straps, saying, "We don't need these anymore." This precious young woman was in full labor, but was being treated as if there was no labor at all. I understood the need to remove the baby's heart monitor, but not the monitor for contractions. She was still fully involved in the birthing process.

As the evening progressed, the doctor made a determination to stop the Pitocin drip so that she could rest for the night. She wanted her lungs to have some time to heal and build up strength. The plan was to begin the drip the next morning and break her water to speed up the process once she had rested.

At one point a nurse came in and noticed my daughter's fingernails. She asked her if they had always been that way and my daughter kind of chuckled and said yes. The nurse left the room and I followed her out of the room. I asked why she had questioned my daughter about her fingernails. Her reply was, "we often see that in Cystic Fibrosis patients". She continued to explain that people with CF often have clubbed finger and toe nails because of poor lung function.

I told my husband and my son what the nurse had told me, then I googled Cystic Fibrosis on my phone. Immediately a photo of a hand of a CF patient appeared and I would have sworn that I was looking at the hand of my daughter.

I read a little farther and realized that missing pieces to a lifelong puzzle were suddenly being revealed as fast as I could perceive them. All the doctors, the allergy medications, the signs of oil in her bowel movements, the coughing all through her childhood, all the symptoms never relenting for any length of time in this young lady's life now began to make sense. Not welcome sense, but at least a fresh understanding of my daughter's condition. All of it lay on the web pages on my phone before me. It was like finally connecting the dots of a long scrambled history.

My baby, now lying in labor, had all the signs of a life threatening illness and though I didn't want to, and tried not to, death was staring me in the face after one passing statement made by a nurse about to leave her shift.

As the night progressed, we sent family and friends home until the morning and I stayed with my daughter and her husband at the hospital that night. I was blessed to be in the delivery room for the births of my son's first two children, so I was very familiar with the progression of labor. I knew from the birth of my son's children that it was common for nurses to come in and out frequently, checking for dilation. It was important to keep a close eye on things as my daughter-in-law progressed in order to give the doctor time to administer an epidural.

This was not the case with my daughter. There was no monitor to view, and my daughter's labor never seemed to diminish. I spent the night looking at my watch, timing contractions. There was no nurse on standby, watching for increased labor activity. Once in a while someone came in because her oxygen alarm was going off, but as far as overseeing labor, she was on her own, as far as the hospital staff were concerned.

I can remember that somewhere around 3:00 am in the morning, my daughter's husband finally lay down in the hospital room from complete exhaustion. My daughter, bless her heart, was concerned about him, whether he was eating and his need for sleep.

As I sat in a chair, slumped over her bed, I too, fought extreme exhaustion. Every five minutes she would slightly whimper and we would know another contraction was coming. I would get up and rub her lower back and it would pass in a minute or so. My biggest fear at this point was accidentally falling asleep. I couldn't leave her alone, not now. This girl had no idea of the next minute or hour. Her whole world had been rocked. In my eyes, at that moment, it felt like she was 12 years old again. She turned to me and said, "Mommy would you come lie by me in bed." My heart gasped inside. My first thought was, "I can't do that, I will surely fall asleep." I was panicking, but she was so little lying in that bed, going through the worst imaginable time of her life. I walked around and crawled into the bed next to her and propped my head up on my hand so that I would remain alert, still feeling slumber pulling at my eyelids. Immediately, pain shot through my back from the awkward position in which I was lying. I thought, "How could I sleep under this kind of pain?" and then I heard in my heart, "Yes, how could you fall asleep under that kind of pain?" and then I knew. As long as I stayed in that position and remained in discomfort, I would stay awake. So I did.

As I reclined there next to my daughter in her hospital bed, rubbing her back every five minutes during contractions and watching her drift off in between, I began to experience something I could not immediately understand. When my daughter would have a contraction, I was focused, grief was put on hold, questions and fears of her future days were set aside as if something or someone took over within me and rose up with exact precision to handle what was needed. As the contraction would end, and Mandy would drift off, a realm would open up to me where I would converse with God, sharing my grief, my fear, and my questions.

Throughout the night I would brush her hair because she found it soothing. This simple act of mothering took me back through the years to remember when she was just a little girl. Tears would fill my eyes as I lay there beside my child. I wept as I was flooded by thoughts of her childlessness and the potential of life threatening lung disease. It was a back and forth communion for over two hours as the room lay silent between labor pains. I and my Father interacted so intimately. I lived again days gone by and precious moments that had passed so long ago all within two hours at my Father's feet.

Our family had been convinced that this child

would be raised from the dead and we prayed with confidence over her belly believing it to be so. As I communed with my Father, He gave me a vision at 3:00 am of baby Alayna being carefully wrapped up in a butter-fly-like cocoon. I watched as each strain of silk wrapped its way around her tiny little body in the womb until every last inch of her was covered. I asked God, "What is going on?" He told me that He had her all safely wrapped up. He showed me that baby Alayna was transitioning into a new realm with Him. There would be no resurrection, there would be no life here, she was going home and I would soon be seeing her lifeless little body enter the world right before my very eyes.

At that moment, he reminded me of the lullaby that Mandy and Nick learned from the moment they found out they were expecting a baby. The song was entitled, Safe and Sound, which would come to mean so much more in the days ahead.

SAFE AND SOUND
Verse 1

*I remember tears streaming down your
   face,*
When I said, "I'll never let you go"
*When all these shadows almost killed
   your light,*
*I remember you said, "don't leave me
   here alone."*
*But all that's dead and gone and passed
   tonight.*

Chorus

Just close your eyes.
The sun is going down.
You'll be alright.
No one can hurt you now.
Come morning light,
You and I'll be safe and sound.

Verse 2

*Don't you dare look out your window,
   Darling.*
Everything's on fire!
*The war outside our door keeps raging
   on!*

49

Brenda Godson

Hold on to this lullaby,
Even when music's gone...gone

Chorus
Just close your eyes.
The sun is going down.
You'll be alright.
No one can hurt you now.
Come morning light,
You and I'll be safe and sound.

God has a way of preparing us long before we face hard things. For months the heavenly Father had my daughter discover this song, learning it and singing it. She and her husband would even play their keyboard and violin, while she would sing it, so they would know it perfectly by the time of the baby's arrival. They planned to sing it to her every night as they put her to bed.

Chapter 5

A few hours passed with contractions coming every four to five minutes. I called the nurse to informed her that someone needed to check my daughter for dilation because I could see the transition taking place. I had to buzz twice before the nurse came. She said there was no need to check my daughter, because the drip had been stopped hours ago. She told me the doctor would come by in the morning and break her water. I demanded that she be checked, because I knew she was transitioning rapidly.

The nurse still tried to persuade me to see the unnecessary need for an exam. I did not relent to push for the simple exam. I knew that no one had checked on her or bothered to monitor the contractions. My quiet little girl never complained once through all that she was experiencing. Only tears would stream down her face due to the intense pain.

About 10 minutes later the nurse came back and said she would check her. She quickly realized that my daughter was fully dilated. Because of the irresponsibility of the hospital staff and the lack of care for my daughter, the circumstances now left us at the end of the road with no one present but my daughter, her husband, and me.

The nurse was totally unprepared. She walked around the room disconnected. I asked, "Is her doctor coming?" She said yes. After a few minutes I asked again, "Is her doctor coming?" My daughter inquired, "Am I getting the epidural?" The nurse replied in the affirmative, but that it might be 30 minutes before it could be administered. I looked at the nurse and pleaded, "She doesn't have 30 minutes." "She is not getting it is she?" I commented. The nurse said, "Probably not." I continued, "Her doctor is not going to make it either, is she?" and the nurse again replied, "Probably not."

Looking at the situation with my daughter now feeling extreme pressure below, her husband nervously pacing, and the nurse still not gloved up and walking around in a daze; I realized that I was going to have to help my daughter deliver her baby. There was not going to be a doctor leading the way and explaining things as we went along. There was not going to be the support that one should have at a horrific time like this.

All of a sudden, there was a shift inside of me. We had a job to do and it was time to get down to business. I lifted up the sheet that covered my daughter and as I looked, the head of the baby was crowning. I told my daughter, "We are going to have to deliver this baby ourselves." She said, "Mommy I can't!" I told her, "Look at me...yes you can...you are strong remember." She looked at me and suddenly I saw it in her eyes. The game had changed and she was positioned and ready to take the field. Fear left its brief residency and courage rose like David stepping on the field with Goliath.

I said, "When you feel that next contract, push." Quickly the next contraction came and the head of the baby was out. I instructed my daughter to push when the next contraction came and the body and legs appeared. The baby arrived just in time for the nurse to finally have her gloves on and reach down as the feet were the only thing left to exit.

A momentary sigh of relief filled the room. The pain was instantly over and Mandy's head fell back to the bed as she took a deep breath, but within seconds that relief left. The pain of a lifeless birth hammered us like a ton of rocks. There on the bed lay Alayna Renee Wilson, 2.5 lbs, 14 inches long, blue and without life. No cry filled the air and no movement identified her arrival, just silence and Alayna lying there motionless. Little Alayna, having received no honor from the staff as she made her way into the world, never having had the opportunity to make her mark or bring laughter to her parents, was now with Jesus and her beautiful but empty body, left for us to view.

Recently, I was told a story by one of my spiritual brothers, who had a vision of the seed of his father falling between his sister and himself. He went to his father and asked him if he had ever cheated on his mother. The father replied, "No, why do you ask?" He told him of the vision and then the father explained they had lost a child in the womb at 5 months. It was painful so they never talked about it. Weeks later my brother had a dream where he went to heaven. While there a young man ran up to him with joy and excitement, telling him how proud he was of my brother and how much he enjoyed watching his life unfold. My brother inquired what had happened to the young man. The man replied, "I am your brother. God took me home because he knew that if I stayed on earth as your brother, I wouldn't have let half the stuff happen to you that you have been through, and all of that was necessary for you to walk in your destiny." Then his heavenly brother told him that he was sorry he hadn't mentioned his name and he told him what his name was. After the dream my brother went to his father and said, "Dad did y'all ever name the baby you lost?" The father said that it was strange he had asked because he and the mother had argued over the name the child would be given, but finally settled on the name the mother wanted. That was the exact name his brother in Heaven used to introduce himself.

There has been a teaching circulated in recent years that a life taken at such a young age, has to be an attack from the enemy. No child should be robbed of his life and destiny before the appointed time. But look at what my brother discovered. Within five months his older brother had lived the entirety of his destiny. His life was not shortened; it was lived!

Some lives end too early. God tells us that the only thing that can shorten one's life is foolishness or wickedness, but who has the full definition of life? Some will affect more people in a short time than others who live a long life only touching a few. None of us know the beginning from the end—only God does. Destiny is measured by God's design, not ours. We have taken the sovereignty of God and tried to make it into something we can understand with our limited understanding, therefore limiting the message of sovereignty.

As the heavens are higher than the earth,
so are my ways higher than you ways
and my thoughts than your thoughts.
Isaiah 55:9

Acceptance of God's sovereignty is not lack of faith! It is faith in action, whatever the outcome. I cannot will my own way into action, because the alternative is too painful to accept, no more than I can accept the outcome without first exercising my faith. In the end, God remains the same. He is not a heartless God with a deaf ear. He is not positioned to impose pain for the sake of His gain. He is sovereign. He sees the beginning and knows the end. He sees all the bends in the river of life that will bring about the greatest return for ALL of mankind. He is not limited by our fears or driven by our agendas. He is God, plain and simple.

Chapter 6

Alayna was quickly taken away to be cleaned up and dressed so she could be brought back for my daughter, her husband, and grandparents to say goodbye. We remained in the room with her as they tended to my daughter's needs following the birth. I stood and observed the tremendous emotional confusion on her face. She was told that her placenta was not coming out. The nurses said it could take two to six hours for it to naturally come out, if not she would be taken into surgery to have it removed. Something new was showing up on my daughter's face; concern of possible surgery to remove the placenta.

After she was settled and my husband had arrived to the room, I made my way down stairs for a brief moment of fresh air. As I sat down on the curb watching the cars pass by, with daylight approaching, I became angry...very angry. My conversation with God went something like this:

"How could you have allowed this to happen? My daughter was treated like a constipated patient and put in the hospital to wait for a bowel movement. She lay there with no care from the staff and I had to help her deliver her baby, because no one took her pregnancy seriously, because she no longer had a viable fetus. How could you allow her to have a baby shower and the next day let her lose her baby, only to have to watch her brother deliver his third healthy child? She has not even had her first! How could you allow her to endure this kind of treatment? How much do you think I am able to handle? What's wrong with you God? This cannot be love!"

Everything around me went mute—traffic, my thoughts, the voices of passersby. I heard God say:

"Who do you think you are? I gave this gift to you. I removed doctors, nurses, staff and others so that you would have

*this precious moment with your daugh-
ter, a moment you will never forget. I
did this for you. It was your honor."*

I began to weep uncontrollably. I realized that
God had sovereignly given us a gift in the
midst of tragedy that would be remembered
forever as we processed through the loss of
one so precious. He had so carefully orches-
trated a moment of history, where two women
and one man would embrace adversity together and overcome with a strength that could
only come from God himself.

My anger turned to praise as I had my eyes
open wider to see the hand of God all through
the midst of adversity and pain. I began to
thank him for the gift and thank him for not
leaving us nor forsaking us. Praise became
my hearts overflow, even in the midst of grief.
My God was in complete control.

I went back up stairs and soon they brought
the body of my daughter and son's precious
Alayna. The Placenta had not yet dislodged

and there was still a potential for surgery, but Amanda held the body of her daughter for the first time.

We looked at her with a deep realization that she was gone. Within minutes God directed my eyes to her nose and how it looked like my daughters. Soon the room shifted and everyone was checking out her feet and noticing they were like her father's. We observed every detail of her tiny body, even her hands and ears and hair. We were all being led by God to embrace her life as well as her death, all at the same time. There were smiles on all our faces as we viewed God's handiwork and how He had woven her parent's features together into this tiny, precious body. She was truly a magnificent work of art, perfect in every way. Our joy was tempered and grief dug deeper by the all to realization that we would never have the opportunity to see her grow up.

Alayna was taken and goodbyes were said. Her parents never requested another time with her, because they knew that she was with Jesus and there was no life in holding on to lifelessness.

Hours later, my daughter said, "Momma, I don't want to have to go through surgery to have the placenta removed. I have been through so much already and so I asked God if maybe it could come out with one good cough."

She got up because she needed to use the bathroom. While sitting on the toilet, she coughed and out it came. We marveled at the swift, practical answer to such a simple prayer. We laughed and cried as we realized God had done exactly what she had asked in such a convenient way.

Alyana, a Tribute to Courage and Destiny

Brenda Godson

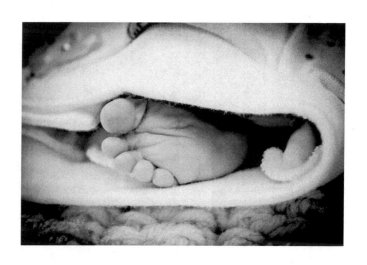

Alyana, a Tribute to Courage and Destiny

Brenda Godson

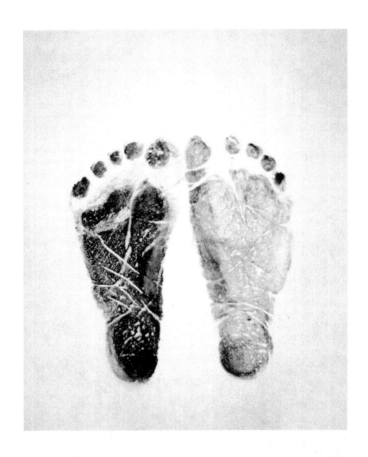

Chapter 7

My daughter had overheard about her possible lung issues, but it really didn't register. She was so focused on her loss, and then the labor that we doubted if she even heard the discussion at all. Before the day was over, a whole new set of doctors were called in to evaluate her condition for a completely different reason than the one which hospitalized her. Within 24 hours a lung specialist was consulted and ordered tests, lung x-rays, breathing analysis, sweat test (CF diagnostics), organ analysis, just to name a few. My daughter was thrown into another major life altering revelation before she had even had time to recover her footing from the first.

After two days of nothing but test, I find her sitting still in the labor and delivery room now undergoing an new onslaught of pressure. She was feeling the loss of all control. Her future was hanging in the balance, and YET... in the midst of extreme adversity, this woman of 24 years was rising above it to show the world what grace in action looked like. She became an amazement to others. Some questioned whether she was even processing anything. They felt she might be in shock or that she really wasn't fully engaged, because they thought she should surely be falling apart.

As the days went by, I watched her and her husband rise and overcome. Her wisdom was beyond her years and her strength beyond most. She entered each moment of concern with careful thought and rose with steadfast conviction. She never once drew attention to herself by embracing a victim mindset or attempting to create a platform for the world to focus on her. She remained gracious and selfless, rarely if ever requesting a thing or allowing anyone to make a fuss over her.
We were placing our faith in the truth of the Psalmist:

He will cover you with his feathers, and under his wings you will find refuge; his faithfulness will be your shield and rampart.
Psalm 91:4

And of the Apostle Paul:

> *But He said to me,*
> *"My grace is sufficient for you,*
> *for my power is made perfect in weakness."*
> *Therefore we will boast all the more gladly*
> *about our weaknesses,*
> *so that Christ's power may rest on us!*
> 2 Corinthians 12:9

Though she was weak, she was strong. Though her body tried to fail her, her God upheld her. Oh the sweetness of Him who loves, cares and never ever forsakes us in our time of need. A caring Father in heaven was now holding her and her husband in the grip of his love.

Preliminary test results arrived which indicated that Cystic Fibrosis was a highly probable diagnosis, but until the sweat test came back, no conclusion was final. The doctors decided that she could go home with follow-up appointments as planned.

The doctor that was called in to consult was also part of God's handiwork. He was the director of pulmonary units in our area, and quickly became intrigued by this girl who had flown under the CF radar for 24 years and was still alive to tell about it. He was instantly provoked to compassion in his first visit with her in the hospital. His specialty was CF and he was taking a very proactive role in her case. He stated she would need a local doctor to spearhead her treatments and to keep close contact with the Cystic Fibrosis Foundation on her behalf. We asked him if he would be willing to take her case and he replied, "I would be honored."

After the doctor left, we were told by the nurse that specialty doctors never allow someone they are treating to remain in another ward where they have to travel to them on their rounds. In the midst of our first visit, this specialist looked into the face of a girl who had just lost her baby. He knew that asking her to leave labor and delivery would be perceived as saying that what just happened was not real.

He knew it was time for her to leave the baby and focus on her health, but he was gracious enough to allow her to remain in labor and deliver until she could more fully heal emotionally and physically. He kindly consented to come to her instead.

Chapter 8

We left the hospital with only a small box of memories from the life of Alayna. Her little foot and hand prints on a mold, her little blanket and other odds and ends. I noticed that everything had a little butterfly on it. Her hat, her bracelet and other things, bringing me back to the vision I had when God had wrapped her up in a butterfly-like cocoon. He was confirming that he had given me that vision. I had not dreamed it because I fell into some emotional low place.

Next to my daughter and her husband, as we walked out of the hospital, was her brother and his wife who was eight months into her own pregnancy, pushing their two other children in a double baby stroller. I watched as my daughter walked next to her husband as he held the little box full of his daughter's little things. Grace reflected like a sunrise over them, encapsulating them in His glory.

God's strength can only be seen in our weakness. Moments when others might say, "How in the world can one bear so much and overcome so much?" God's strength dials up His grace and one walks in the atmosphere of the supernatural provision way above normal to show that God is real. He is able to do exceedingly and abundantly more than we could ask or ever dream.

Chapter 9

We arrived to my house to get my daughter and her husband settled in to the back bedroom. They had decided they needed some time before going home to face an empty house.

For the next weeks, we arose each morning, plowing through the day with grace as the only thing keeping us from drowning in the sorrow of the loss. For others life goes on—baby showers, barbecues, new houses, job interviews—we can only watch from the refuge of our compound, feeling that if life as usual comes flooding back too soon we will be swept away by the senseless pursuit of business as usual.

We honestly can't engage with others, because there is too much to wade through. God is good to carefully take us by the hand and lead us through every bend in this painful river. The waves of grief crash on the shores of our hearts so fast and hard that there seems no time to even take a breath. Two worlds collided with a thunderous contrasting impact on us. One world encompasses the deep loss of Alayna. The other focuses out attention on the joy of the coming arrival of Phoebe, my son's new child.

We were gripped by fear of how to stand, but aware with the knowledge that grief and joy will soon take up the same place in time. Torn apart, yet held together by an invisible benevolent force; broken, yet steadfast. Fearful, yet confident; feeling alone, yet knowing we are not.

Within 24 hours of leaving the hospital, my daughter began to lactate. Momentarily, It caused her to weep. She experienced how painful it is to be producing milk and have no baby to feed. But grace enveloped her again as we wrapped her tightly to restrict the production. We packed her with cold compresses to relieve some of the pain. Day after day, this was a constant reminder of having birthed a baby, yet there was no baby to hold. My daughter and her husband continued to ride the waves like skilled surfers maneuvering through the obstacles of grief and loss.

Within a week, we began to discuss Cystic Fibrosis. My daughter decided to do a little research on her own. She discovered the gravity of what possibly lied before her. Later that day, she came outside to sit by me and said momma, "I want to play you a song. Its my new theme song...because I'm gonna fight this." Here is her song:

ROAR!

I used to bite my tongue and hold my breath
Scared to rock the boat and make a mess
So I sat quietly, agreed politely
I guess that I forgot I had a choice
I let you push me past the breaking point
I stood for nothing, so I fell for everything

You held me down, but I got up
Already brushing off the dust
You hear my voice, you hear that sound
Like thunder gonna shake the ground

Brenda Godson

You held me down, but I got up
Get ready cause I've had enough
I see it all, I see it now

I've got the eye of the tiger, a fighter,
dancing through the fire
Cause I am a champion
and you're gonna hear me roar
Louder, louder than a lion
Cause I am a champion
and you're gonna hear me roar
You're gonna hear me roar

Now I'm floating like a butterfly
Stinging like a bee I earned my stripes
I went from zero, to my own hero
You held me down but I got up
Already brushing off the dust
You hear my voice, you hear that sound
Like thunder gonna shake the ground
You held me down, but I got up
Get ready cause I've had enough
I see it all I see it now

Alyana, a Tribute to Courage and Destiny

I got the eye of the tiger a fighter,
dancing through the fire
Cause I am a champion,
and you're gonna hear me roar
Louder, louder than a lion
Cause I am a champion
and you're gonna hear me roar!

(Lyrics by Katy Perry, WB Music Corp.)

Within a few hours, she had decided that circumstances were not going to hold her down, because she had the heart of a champion.
I looked at her and said that she was one of the most amazing women I had ever known. She was raising the bar for everyone around her and truly showing a life of complete dependence on God.

As I watched her, I also saw a man walking beside her, whom God had sent to us only a few years ago to be her husband, walk in total sacrificial love and grace. He cared for her heart as if she were a china doll and declared that whatever it took to pursue her care he would see to it that it was done. It didn't matter what he had to do—work two jobs or even sell his blood—he would be the man that she could depend on as they both depended on God. I loved watching this tender love exchange. Incredible grief that would drive some couples apart, drew them even closer together with God.

A week and a half after getting home, no one expected to see them at church. Because we are in leadership of a local church, all of our children are on the worship team. That morning I am getting ready for church and she tells me that her husband and her are going with us. At the gathering of the body they both take positions on the platform just two weeks after the loss of their child, and the multiple tests and CF concern, with instruments in hand to worship their God whom they love and praise in the midst of it all. At the end my daughter leads us in Amazing Grace...it covers me... through tears and the whole room is captivated by the presence and beauty of God. It was one of the most powerful displays of God's amazing grace I have ever witnessed. Many were touched that day by what God had done and was doing.

We move forward into the second week at home and I am helping my daughter and son-in-law with cremation details, picking out urns, looking for engravers, handling autopsy reports; all the while, my daughter is taking breathing treatments three times a day, having chest compressions twice a day and still healing from the birth and loss, never ever complaining. We sing her song with her and now it is becoming ours. I am getting calls from family and friends telling us that they are being touched mightily by the example of our family as we move through this crisis. My brother called to say he had been so touched by Alayna's story. He said God had shown him he valued things in his life more than people. He told me he was selling everything he didn't need and was going to use the money to bring their second adoptive child home from Africa. Because of Alayna, he had began to look at situations that had long since angered and frustrated him in a whole new light. Our story had really impacted him and his family. So many expressed marvel at how we handled these things, questioning how we endured and seeing the hand of God at work.

Over and over again, we were hearing reports of lives touched through the life of a child that never took a breath in this life. My daughter and her husband were viewed as living testimonies and models of courage that most people only hope to be. God was using our lives to touch others as we walked together through the trials and continued dwell in the presence of the absolute peace in God.

Mandy's first appointment at the pulmonologist arrived and we would soon receive the results of all of the tests. Her doctor went meticulously through each result until he arrived at the sweat test. CF patients usually run between 60 and 200. My daughter's score was 136. The doctor began to talk with us about the days ahead. He personally made a call to the CF Foundational Director and set up an appointment for my daughter to have a full assessment and put a treatment plan in place. He sat with us and slowly answered all of our questions, never creating an atmosphere of fear. Within 48 hours after leaving his office, my daughter received a call back from him personally on a Saturday to see if she had heard from the foundation. He told her to keep his personal number and call him on his cell if she didn't hear anything by Monday. He had a passion for my daughter's life and we felt he was God's sent-one to all of us.

My daughter has began the process of treating her CF. We know that at anytime her healing could completely manifest, but we will praise God and stand fast with grace as our carrier and faith in the truth that whatever comes our way, our God is Greater!

Chapter 10

When suffering invades our lives, our first response is often, why me. We see the trial as an attack and attempt to reason ourselves out it. We become angry, discouraged or withdraw all together, feeling cheated or robbed, chastened or even orphaned. In the midst of the accounts recorded in this book, God showed me that grief and joy can occupy the same space and time. In order to embrace joy, we must be willing to acknowledge grief.

With the coming arrival of my second granddaughter any day, I was confronted with the pain of having to go back to the same hospital where two weeks earlier I had lost a grandchild, yet to watch the birth of another. Joyous, yes! Painful, yes! One died and one will live. One will have life and one will have not. But God...but God is the same, yesterday today and forever.

The time arrived when the call to go to the hospital came. I made my way to the Labor and Delivery area for the second time in two weeks, first for death, now for life. My heart was racing and my emotions were churning to the point of physical illness, but still grace, grace, grace.

It would not be known for hours, that this would be a false alarm. Phoebe was not due for another week and her parents would eventually be sent home after the nurses confirmed the presence of false labor. Of chorus, as far as we were concerned, all signs were present that labor was underway and I was by no means ready to watch her entrance, so soon after the death of Alayna.

Not hours before, I sat by a rivers edge processing the new information that some friends had deceived me. In the worst time of my life, I uncovered a deception that was lurking in the background all this time. I was devastated. I began making phone calls to get to the bottom of it with grace and mercy now the farthest thing from my mind. I felt betrayed and lonely, tired and empty.

As I approached the hospital, I thought about my friends, and how hurt I was. It seemed that every emotional battle was coming one after the other, and soon I would be standing in the delivery room to face yet another. For a moment I thought about people who cut themselves and could actually understand their pain. The pain inside can build to the point where cutting seems like a logical, viable option to relieve the building pressure of extreme stress. Then, within moments, God dialed up the grace and dampened the pain, allowing some relief and power to come so I can move each foot a step closer towards the hospital.

Battles confronted me on all fronts; finances, relationships, life, death and faulty belief systems. I no longer wondered how much I can take because I have no strength to hold on to anything anymore.

Aaron Shust has a song called "Satisfy". The words say that I find everything I need in God. No one can embrace that dependence until they can no longer obtain it with their own hands. When everything in your life is threatened—lives taken, peace threatened, grief standing like a wrecking ball at the door of your heart—one will find themselves, at the feet of Jesus crying out for help and will find it. The questions are gone, feelings of entitlement are gone, anger is gone, and our thirst is quenched by the cup we have now agreed to drink, whatever the outcome, because we now rest solely in the capable hands of Jesus both now and forever. We no longer declare life to be unfair, because the cup has carried to our inner man the understanding that our life is not our own and we have chosen to not just talk about being dead to self, but are dead to self. We don't scream for justice or toil for more, because we have surrendered to a higher place, one above this world at the right hand of our Father in Christ. Our sufferings are no longer our sufferings, as we are not our own possessions. We recognize that whatever comes our way, Christ came first way ahead of time. He has already taken the pain and loss from anything that comes.

I remember at one point saying, "Jesus, make yourself known, prove that your word is true and raise this baby from the dead." Later God told me, "I have nothing to prove to you. You are mine now and are seated with me. The only proof that is needed is for those that are yet to believe." He proposed a question to me, asking what I would do if He didn't heal my grandchild and daughter? Paul who had a "thorn in his flesh" and was told that God's grace was sufficient and that the thorn would not be removed.

Stephen was not spared from being stoned to death as the very first martyr. John was boiled in oil. Joseph was sold into slavery. All of these were key people used by God to reach a people group through their willingness to suffer for the message of the Kingdom.

God asked me if I would drink of the cup I was holding, regardless of the outcome? Would we allow our family to suffer for the opportunity to model sufficient grace?

God's word says, if my people, who are called by my name, will humble themselves...
Was I willing to embrace humility at all cost, surrendering all of my rights and desires to the point of death to answer a higher call? My answer again was Yes!!! Whatever may come my way in Him, and Him alone, I place my trust.

Alayna's ashes were scattered in the ocean. Roses were placed on the surf by each person who attended the service. Butterflies were released acknowledging that she had transitioned not only in birth, but in life, to be with Jesus until we all arrived together safe and sound. We will all go on with her memory in our hearts until we see her again, but until that time we will fight with the heart of a champion until our days are done here.

Alayna has had an impact that has changed history and has probably lived out more of her destiny in 7 months than many live in a lifetime. She was a sent-one, sent to declare the message of the Kingdom and show light on an illness that had gone undetected for 24 years. She brought family together as her life readjusted our priorities and put our eyes of the Father in full view. She was loved, will forever be loved, and now sits as a member of the great cloud of witnesses cheering on her family as we finish the remainder of our time on earth. I am forever grateful to have known her and forever grateful for the impact that she has made in my life. She has taught me that life is so precious and far more valuable than things.

Chapter 11

After laying Alayna's body to rest at sea, I was up bright and early the next morning to make my way to the hospital once again. This was to be the day of Phoebe's arrival.

Here I am, on the set of the same scene again, holding the same script in my hands, but this time the cast members were different. There seemed to be people everywhere I looked—two nurses, one midwife, a doctor, two grandmothers, a one sister and a husband. Never for one moment was the expectant mother alone.

The nurses moved about with precision as if they were on a mission, reading monitor tapes, helping at every turn and fetching any request from my daughter-in-law.

The midwife stood constant watch, comforting, checking for dilation, wiping the expectant mother's forehead with a damp cloth, putting her hair up out of her face, and breathing with her during every contraction. The doctor came in and out, always making sure she was there in plenty of time to assist in the live birth.

I watched as the scene unfolded before my eyes. I had no part in this scene, but to just sit and observe. Two worlds were coming into full view, one of justice and the other of injustice. The reality of the two was suffocating, polar opposites. Dignity and honor versus dishonor and neglect in the other.

This was a God moment...I knew it. He was showing me the condition of man on two real levels. The question would be, what would the sides do with where they were positioned? Would the dishonored still honor and the honored honor back? Could I myself, stand within three weeks and look injustice in the face and still hold tight to the Heart of the Father for humanity? Could I say without gritting my teeth, "Lord, forgive them, for they know not what they do (and have done)?"

These were the very same doctors, midwife and nurses that left my daughter without care, just weeks before. The test was, can I stand here without exploding and watch them display their skills and talents differently because this mother carries a living fetus?

I was reminded of my second trip to Africa. Because it was an international flight, each seat had its own TV monitor. Before take-off, on Delta, there was a brief introduction of how the plane prepares itself for takeoff. The plane points it's nose into the direction of the wind and as it builds up speed, the wind comes up under the wings and gives it lift. If it tried the same takeoff with the wind to its rear, it would plow nose first into the pavement.

We cannot run from the winds of adversity. That which pushes against you is the very thing which gives you lift. It is the only way of reaching higher heights.

Phoebe was born with the assistance of a full staff. Joy filled the room upon her arrival and upon hearing her first cry.

My daughter, who had just buried her baby the day before, was texting her brother and me, checking on the progress and sending her blessings. She had some of the natural feelings that one would expect; sadness for herself and her husband, but joy for her brother. She and her husband even brought coffee to everyone downstairs as she couldn't yet bring herself to come upstairs in the midst of all that was happening. I kept looking at her through the eyes of compassion, waiting for the floodgate of anger to burst, but all I saw was grace and more grace as she turned into the wind.

The following day, I told her I was heading up to the hospital to make a quick visit and she as well as her husband agreed to go with me. This was huge, because no one would have expected her to be able to do such a selfless thing so soon after her own loss. If the truth be told, few others would have done it themselves. There, clothed in humility, grace and compassion they both put others above themselves. They turned their hearts again, into the winds of adversity, fueled with grace and ready for liftoff to yet another destination.

Chapter 12

So many people reach the end of their own ability and say, "I have done all I can emotionally or physically do, I can do no more!" They remain stagnant in their growth.

> *I can do all things through*
> *Christ who strengthens me.*
>
> Philippians 4:13

This is a great verse to quote when we are on a road to greater strength, better job or building a bigger empire for ourselves. It is a great verse for cheering us on to the greater things of life. Bill Johnson said, *"God warned people about building kingdoms for themselves. All that we are given is for the equipping and serving of others, not self."*

With every action there is always a reaction or cause and effect. I must examine my thoughts before they become actions, because the reactions, which automatically follow, can either bring about life or further harm to others.

I remember my spiritual Father, Jack Taylor, saying one day that the greater always includes the lesser, but the lesser never includes the greater.

The greater love or expression of God himself is the laying down of one's life as shown in John 15:13. *Greater love has no man than this; to lay down one's life for one's friends.*

Lay it down...no need to exalt oneself to the forefront, no need to build up oneself. It means humility, "not I, but you God." He is the Greater, but in Him all is included without fear of exclusion. I can willingly embrace the cause of others as I know that my heart is not one of poverty, but of sonship.

I read of Jesus dying on the cross for a totally undeserving world. Even though none deserved it, he died anyway. I saw in my children a man and a woman embracing the true essence of Jesus, operating in abandonment to an undeserving system. Grace was leading them and lifting them higher.

Neither of them fully realized the altitude to which they were climbing as the clouds of grief still cover the landscape below. But soon they would burst through the clouds to see a new season full of the new sights and sounds of a King and His Kingdom that has arrived on the scene of their life in all His glory. This is what is established in the hearts of those willing to take the road of the cross.

Jesus himself suffered in the hours before his death. Knowing how hard his cross would be and the road that lie before him, his physical body began to bleed hours before it was broken. As he sweat and wept in the garden, even in those hours, his blood was spilled through the pores in his skin, as the trauma of what lay ahead drew near.

There is a building of pressure within the heart of man that is sensitive to God's heart. Things can change with great speed and intensity. It is a pressure like none other, if one desires to discern it. It is discerned only by facing adversity and embracing the birth pains of the falling away of oneself to see the establishment of the Kingdom of God.

Many say Jesus suffered so I wouldn't have to, but nothing of that is scriptural. He actually tells us to pick up "our" cross and not just the one we hang around our neck, but the one where we die with Him. It is the cross where self hangs overshadowed and consumed by a another man...a King for all the world to see.

There are no accolades for mortal man, but praises for a King. The individual becomes a footstool for the honored King to take his rightful place. Hearts are lowly in the presence of such greatness and majesty. Honor seems only fitting to the One who created the heavens and the universe. In such an atmosphere, one is quick to dismiss the need for attention, as one's whole being is captivated and completely distracted by someone far greater than themselves. O, how close we are to the world bowing its' knees at the coming of the greatest time in History. I am blessed not to praise a man and woman for their own strength, but to witness their place on the cross, where Jesus has shown himself yet again.

I close with one last story told by my biological brother from a sermon he heard years ago: A pastor told of when he was young of how he and his sister always played monopoly. He said that she always beat him and took everything he had. Finally one day he decided he would beat her for once. So he played the game with precision and took every dime and property she had. After the game was over he asked her what she thought about him now. She said..."it doesn't matter; it all goes back in the box anyway."

Money, things, busyness, power, cars, houses and all the other things we take stock in will go right back in the box, but life lives on through the heart of every believer, both here and eternity to come.

About Amanda & Nick

Amanda and Nick married in 2011 and currently living in Palm Bay, Florida. Amanda is employed by Dimensions Ministries as a part time bookkeeper and Nick is an IT Specialist, contracted to NASA.

Both have a great love for family as well as traveling when time permits. Amanda continues to be an advocate for her health and is diligently working on exercise and nutrition to fight the good fight against Cystic Fibrosis.